PILLARS

OF

SAND

Poems made from Dreams

by

J. T. BENNETT

Published by J.T. Bennett
Nielsen ISBN: 978-0-9575896-2-9
Copyright Holder© 2014
First Edition

The moral right of the author has been asserted. The
characters and events portrayed in this book are
fictitious. Any similarity to real persons, living or dead is
coincidental and not intended by the author.

Author's Website;
http://jtbennettauthor.wix.com/fourcorners

Dedication.

The year of the publication of this work, 2014, is the Centenary. It has been 100 years since the start of the First World War.

I have written this book in commemoration of those who have suffered in turbulent times and lost their lives in combat, as well as for those who have been left behind.

For my Dad.

Pillars of Sand

Poems made from Dreams

The Lily

June 24, 2009

Draped elegantly and proud, all slender and white,

the Stargazer Lily, with its sweet perfume—

not a flower could compare, not a star in the night.

Poppies red, like spots across the meadow,

a folded cloth,

a day to remember.

Suits and arms; medals shiny.

Why mourn when the poppies dance so prettily in the

wind,

and the lilies lie, all slender and proud?

And then, like a star, they open up...and there you are!

All white, pure and new,

like the spring; like the new morning.

CONTENTS

Introduction:

The Lily

PART ONE

Poems & Dreams...

PART TWO

Those Who Are Left Behind...

PART ONE: Poems & Dreams.

Pillars of Sand

June 2010

Pillars of sand, standing tall and erect,

overlooking the desert, a pavilion; a monument; a place

of respect.

Eyes of the future...

Feeling the fear of the people,

sensing the deeds of tomorrow,

warning them; leading them; guiding their way.

Freedom...

Freedom must be fought for.

Pillars of sand stand tall.

Corners collapse and disperse into the desert.

Fear running free...

Knives follow sharp...

Cutting and lunging,

followed by the eyes and teeth of young children.

A war...

Dead men are free.

Like pillars of sand, monuments stand,

their graves demand

that place of respect.

The Fallen

July 22, 2014

The earth moans,

corpses stare,

their eyes empty tunnels; absent; departed.

Scenes held still; captions; imprisoned.

They are the fallen, the photo from the pocket; the

father, the lover.

Rain pelts down...ammunition firing,

large pellets; droplets, spots on soft casings of empty

shells,

with sweat and blood mingles.

It runs in pinkish rivers, beneath camouflage wrappers;

the inner remains of brave, dead men.

Dawn breaks. The sun rises, but nothing stirs.

Still is all but the tall grass as it dances in the morning
breeze.

Miles away, as the cock crows; birds sing; children play.

Unaware, their fields are tainted with acres of death on
the summer's day.

The sun reaches out in the clear blue sky as scorching,
sweltering carcasses stiffen,
their rigid figures covered in flies,
reeking; putrid, rotting eyes.

Summer ends, and autumn tarnishes the bloody
ground.

Wind blows; leaves dance and scurry around.

An amber bed; crisp with colours, dead and deepening.

Gales rage like a torrent, cold as ice.

The soil is their bed, their slumber, their camouflage

from the shells in life.

Snow falls softly: a gentle tickle; a white sheet of linen;

covered, protected, never forgotten.

Spring dawns, draws breath.

Shoots of birth stretch forth through furrows of

darkness.

Blackness, hard soil deepened with gloomy madness,

now awakens; stillness from sleep.

A sprout, a bud, bursts forth, arises;

spurting; erupting, emerging in warmth;

burrowing, softening;

nestling, a new beginning...

A life lost; a love remembered...will always live on.

They Have Gone

September 27, 2014

Voices:

whispering,

calling...

Beneath the dry earth,

beneath the soft grass:

Those who are forgotten.

"We are gone."

Monuments: cold, empty,

without soul.

Stone upon stone,

words engraved:

"Beloved,"

"Remembered,"

"Never to be forgotten."

They have gone.

They have gone.

Brave Young Things

July 26, 2014

Together they ran, brave young things,

trembling, their hearts beating fast,
thinking of home, thinking of...anything—
no time left, no breath to breathe, no choice.

Smells sickening: fear, blood, death.
Hearts drumming, beating.
Bullets firing.
Sheets of rain.
Red-faced, a cold sweat.
Dropping like flies...
Together they fell in the cold, dark night.

I saw him; his eyes pleading, his body shaking,

weakening fast.

The sky was alive; chaos surrounded him.

Together they ran, those brave young things,

in the cold, dark night.

Above wept the heavens; the earth downed their blood.

Hollow Man

December 17, 2012

With sinister eyes, he walks sombrely,

obscure in his long, black coat.

The traffic stops for him, and he stands before us, a

shrouded figure,

threatening and concealed in the shadows of the night.

He sits on the roadside with a defenceless animal.

Without conscience, he breaks its neck.

Snap! It cracks in one swift, cruel *crunch.*

The radio...

Ten years of sufferance, the Western wall.

Chernobyl bleeds.

Snap! Crack! He strikes the blow again.

A shiver runs down my spine.

Didn't this happen before?

He stands up, the hollow man,

   Then he walks away, like a tall, dark shadow.

Fly Away from Here

September 2014

Anger building,

hurtful words, a place to crawl.

Here again, that dreaded day.

The week has been brewing.

Slam the door; leave me hurting, crying,

confused, broken.

Tears fall on furrowed ground

as I walk to the fallen tree.

I cannot forget your startled eyes.

Head in hands,

you sat upon the bed,

your clothes empty, your face invisible.

My dreams are your dreams. I realise that now:

the war, the death, the violence.

I tremble when I hear their voices,

roaring loudly, in good cheer.

I wish they'd leave him,

those drunken soldiers,

leave him to sleep away his fear.

Eyes Peering

September 2014

Eyes peering down,

surveying us.

I look up from our sleeping bed.

He has gone.

My heart is racing.

I am ashamed.

Oh, how I need him now.

Morning comes; hands wet, face in denial.

A stain of blood covers the bed; he's gone.

She stands at the bedpost, asking for money,

pointing to limbs hidden beneath the mattress.

Blood drips from my hands.

She wants her pound of flesh.

He returns; a faceless body, enigmatic and obscure.

The mattress is torn, imbalanced, bumpy,

Body parts force their way out from beneath us,

reaching, pointing, grasping.

She pulls decapitated limbs from the mattress.

I beg her to stop.

A finger pokes roughly into my back.

Then all is revealed.

Water trickles over my hands,

a gentle cleansing,

Delicate drops and scented soap,

purifying, colourful, watery hues of scarlet and blue.

Like a Piece of Meat

February 2012

Two of us tried to lure him.

Danger!
The fear wouldn't go away.
It was always you he wanted, until that day.
Then I feared what would become of me.

And like a piece of meat, I gnawed it down to the bone,
Blood oozed out and it grew to become part of me.

What I'd done, and what I'd planned to do was beyond
my own understanding.
All thought and all reasoning had slipped through the
door.
What I now wanted could not compare

with how I felt: the need to confess I was in love with a

man who could not love, could not care.

Deep in my thoughts, I walked into a barn.

I glanced all around me at the crowds of people, at the

guns, at the soldiers.

The lights were dim, the air was thin,

Screams bellowed everywhere;

like an alarm, they woke me.

My heart triggered fast.

I heard a gun blast.

I was too helpless, too terrified to speak.

The soldiers kept their promise and drew back.

As they walked to the doorway, the silence creaked.

The room whispered.

The meat I held fell.

Something was hurled into the barn,

It fell around our feet, hissing and smoking,

a cloudy mist of choking; it was gas.

A woman cried out between gasps and spluttering.

No one answered.

The room whispered again...

While evil breathes, only the good die.

This Is My Fight

September 2014

A new life; a dream...

With nothing but our clothes on our backs,

with only trust for our shroud, we followed them...to a

new country.

Living crowded among others,

in darkness, in poverty: in a strange building of

antiquities.

Outside in the street, the sun glares in my eyes: blue

tones, fluffy clouds, warm air.

The bazaar is busy.

Spices flow, aromatic and fragrant.

Fabric is displayed in a menagerie of shades, hues and

pigments: the colours of the rainbow.

The cobalt sea is mere yards away.

Where's my camera now?

I walk the road, far from the stone building, far past the
thin windows,
harbouring secret thoughts——to go home, to be...free.

Inside a building, I hear chanting.

Holy men, cross-legged, sit on stone floors.

I hear humming, tunes of familiar songs from years ago,
melodies of another lifetime.

I cannot go home, not now.

For this is my fight, my wish.

I am one of them now.

The road is long, the crowds thick, everything busy.

    Vacant eyes look up at me.

Crowds Gather

February 11, 2012

Crowds gather...

Children scream above the hustle and bustle.

Women wail.

I am separated,

frightened by sounds I hear; words I don't understand.

Confusion...

I realize where my priorities lie.

Trucks, cars, vans, and horse-drawn carts,

piled high with worldly possessions.

The road is blocked.

A menagerie of colours and objects wind their way

slowly along the road ahead...

a caravanserai in the desert.

Searching...

My last chance to find you before it's too late.

The ice rink, the magician...

The chosen venue? The Southern Seat.

Confusion! Panic!

Rushing furiously, searching frantically.

Entertainment? Speeches.

My watch weighs heavy.

I hear it ticking...

Escape!

Plane Crash

February 2012

An uneasy feeling.

Thunderous sounds dominate the sky;

An enormous object; lights sparking;

declining; diving, plummeting down.

My stomach turns: sickness, foreboding,

Intense empathy brims my heart.

Are they my emotions?

I shake and tremble,

When the feeling upwells; surging, rising,

"Run!" they shout.

A darkened sky: the enormous object, ascending down.

Earth shudders.

In fear, we run across barren land.

In silence, we wait:

Heads in hands, emotions immense, fear penetrating.

Five seconds are like minutes,

The plane descends.

It deafens: thundering, revolving, whistling, subsiding,

as I witness their terror, their pain and crushing

emotions.

Such a large vessel; it frightens and moves me.

Small fragments leave the body, fly everywhere.

Others fall heavy, like huge tin cans,

burying them into sand.

Then comes the bulk, the body.

Like rain, people fall from the sky.

Behind other sounds, their terrified screams are pathetic

and weak.

With frightened eyes and stolen breath, they fly.

Nose-down, it crashes, breaking in two,

thundering as it hits the ground.

The earth shudders and moves.

Sparks fly as parts *crack;* dust disperses.

I see a blaze; small fires; arms thrashing, flailing;

burning embers: black,

scorching, bodies of glowing ash.

We run, as fast as we can from screams and explosions,

leaving behind us...

a ticking bomb.

Sacrificing Our Children's Future

2014

Afraid of my vision, I hid underground.

It was hard to distinguish the past from the future,
So much was now how it used to be...

I was in a dark cave.

I knew who those men were, those standing before me.

The bright lights that glowed above their heads told me

they were not real men; they were merely...symbolic.

They were cave-like figures; they represented something.

I almost recognised the symbols and signs, those telling

marks upon the walls.

These men were sacrificing children in secret.

Dozens of boys were huddled together.

They hid their faces, frightened when the men came to

take them away, one boy at a time.

I watched them cling to each other.

They were of different races, different religions,

but that didn't matter to them—not in that moment.

What is the meaning of my dream? We are sacrificing

our children's future?

Shalom

April 2012

Uniforms and guns;

long, dusty coats;

in groups they walk together; smiling and greeting.

I don't walk away.

Rather, I greet them politely,

albeit with fear and uncertainty,

My stomach ties in knots.

Alone I walk past them, repeating their greetings,

wondering if it's wise to continue.

Down the road this continues, different races and

cultures,

but I can't understand anyone.

"Shalom, Shalom..."

What does it mean?

I repeated the greeting in my mixed-up dream.

What are they doing? What's going on?

Is it a war I see beginning before me, and why has it

begun?

Shalom, I discovered means "peace."

We're Free Now

December 2012

Guns fire; they blast.

We run so fast.

We're free now!

Still, we share our food—a bite, a taste—and we pass it

on.

In rags,

like children, our bodies are small and thin.

We're cold; so cold,

Our dark eyes desperate; afraid and weary.

We run away, away from memories of blood and battle;

from recollections of pain and sickening death.

A boy without legs shares an apple with us.

He isn't cold.

He takes us to a room. There is a chair and a fire.

We're not certain why.

A woman is cooking.

We realize she's someone's mum. Time has gone by.

She's just like us: her hair dirty, her clothes untidy.

A baby plays with photographs, discs holding memories

of times gone by.

We look through them, remembering a different world,

a world with love, filled with colours and sweet smells.

"Please play this disc," we ask. "We want to remember.

We want to see colours, to see moving pictures."

She plays it.

The fear leaves us; we feel comfort.

The fire goes out, but we are no longer cold, no longer

hungry.

We hear weeping, loved ones praying.

We'll meet again, in a different world: a world of comfort, a world of love.

Innocence

February 2007

A deep blue ocean.

A ship docked.

Swirling madness, she raced forward,

wheels beneath her.

She gripped tightly; a young girl held her waist,

her long, dark hair flowing freely: an innocent child.

I gasped in horror.

The woman raced through the gap in the barriers,

plummeting through cold depths,

submerging like the *Titanic*.

I watched their bodies sinking,

deeper and deeper.

A scream!

Startled, 1 jumped.

1 realized it was my own voice.

"Save the girl!" 1 cried.

Before my eyes, two bodies were dragged from the water.

She was alive, the girl, the "innocent," 1 thought.

Wrapped in a blanket, she was carried away, her long,

dark hair dripping.

She turned and smiled at me.

She wasn't young; she was a grown woman.

And 1 could see in her eyes that she wasn't innocent at

all...

She was...evil.

The Road Ahead

January 3, 2010

A hot sun; a bumpy road;

blue, cobalt seas, white beaches, and palm trees;

the mountainside: lush and tropical.

The road ahead was blocked; the car slowed down.

Men approached, and we were guided, ever so slowly.

Flanking each side of the road, bodies lie in the mud,

helpless, bleeding, dying, dead.

Still in their swimsuits, still with their thoughts:

at the pool, at the bar, the singer last night, the dancer,

the man with the guitar...

Eyes glazed, they stared blankly,

a horrific scene within them, replaying like a movie on rewind...again and again.

The Lady in the Mirror

2009

An old house bought by an old friend.

A party of guests celebrate an occasion:

cocktails after dinner, congratulations, applause,

merriments.

Explore her new home.

We followed our host from room to room,

each empty; shabby.

They walked back,

and I wandered alone to an open doorway.

An overwhelming aura distressed me: emptiness,

loneliness, sadness.

I was shaken.

I sensed I'd been there before: some cruel déjà vu.

The room was painted and papered in black and white: squares and rectangles; clear, sharp lines; an art deco design.

Furniture, clocks, pictures, and books surrounded me.

A picture of a woman stood out.

Her short, black hair was styled in a bob.

She blinked.

She's...alive?

I stood back, afraid.

She looked at me.

Did I imagine it?

Near the other doorway, at the end of the room, I saw her again.

She looked behind me. I turned.

On the walls were dozens of pictures of her.

Black, inky tears ran down her cheeks.

She looked back at me through the deco mirror, where my image had disappeared.

The Letter

(The Lady in the Mirror Part II)

2011

I'm sure I've been here many times before:

The house, the stairs, the door,

the light, the room...

They're memories,

but one and together, they complete the jigsaw, for the

first time.

Beyond the door is a cluttered attic room.

It's small, furnished with a writing desk, a lamp, and

stacks of books.

Objects fill the surfaces and lie scattered on the floor.

Dust is settled in a thick blanket, cobwebs spun large.

On the wall hangs a picture of a woman I've seen before;

an unhappy woman;

lonely, lost, empty;

her short, black hair cut in a bob.

I look at the picture curiously.

Below it on the desk, a book lies open.

On the page, I see a letter.

My dream begins to fade...

The dream fades, and I don't get my answers, but I recall that the letter suggested I had some connection to the woman. I don't know what house held that room, but the book was a Bible, with family names written inside it.

I have had the dream about the attic room many times before; I am sure if I delve any further, I will find the inevitable skeletons in the closet. Until now, though, I haven't had another dream of the same woman, nor in the attic. Maybe this is my answer after all.

The Polished Surface

(Dream Three, conclusion to "The Lady in the Mirror" and "The
Letter")

Dedicated to Harry.

September 2014.

A polished table set for tea: two cups, two saucers.

A tall window,

curtains drawn back: a view.

On two upholstered chairs, they waited.

Handwritten words: postcards,

a letter opened on the polished surface.

Against the teapot, a telegram stands, unread.

The sun sets, but tomorrow it will rise again.

I look through the window, afraid that one day I will

forget your face.

The teapot is full, but the cups are empty.

I remembered you, just like I said I would.

The curtains are drawn,

the letter is open...

Tears fall slowly on polished wood.

Beyond the shadows,

beneath the timbers...

dust and cobwebs gather there.

A memory is held captive,

amongst clutter, books, and floorboards bare.

They lay upon her polished desk, those handwritten

words,

beneath her interlaced fingertips.

Her eyes meet the cut glass in the decorative mirror,

Her tears in droplets fall,

the lady in black.

Statues

2008

A little girl, a tiny dancer, pirouettes in her ballet
clothes.
She dances through the open doorway of a department
store.

It is dark outside; the lights are off.
The staff has gone home.
Music plays, and the little girl dances happily through
the main entrance.

Beneath the escalators stands a group of mannequins.
Dark silhouettes rise, tall in the shadows.

She twirls and dances around them, looking up at their
tall, shadowy shapes.
To her, they are giants.
The streetlight casts a torch, a gleam of light upon them.
She can just see their smooth, chiselled faces.
Their bodies thin and moulded; their bones blunt and
pointed,
as they move to the music, stiffly, gawkily.

Their tall bodies follow each other in repetition;
rigid arms and legs follow, back and forth.
Turning together, they just miss the girl, who seems
much smaller than she did before.
They march like an army of soldiers, towering above her.
To the little girl, it's just a fashion show.

A mannequin picks up a wooden box; a ballerina music
box.
He gives it to the girl.

Inside are three medallions.

He takes one from it and places it around her neck.

What is the meaning of my dream? Am I the girl, the ballerina in the music box? The mannequins are soldiers, the medallions medals. As children, we are blissfully unaware of war...and of our future.

PART TWO: Those who are left behind.

Fly Away

2004

Fly away, flighty little things. Fly away!

I shall chase you until the swirling breeze catches my

breath no more. Fly away!

Your crispness awakens my buried heart, as I tread

across the soft, thick bed of our love underfoot.

Memories and shadows of our past hide and gather

behind each tree,

while distant echoes carry soft laughter and happiness.

It was there that I lay in your arms, on that deep bed of

leaves,

that later frolicked around us, dancing in the breeze...

tickling your nose, then catching in your hair,

then forming around your nakedness...

Fly away, flighty little things. Fly away!

I shall search for you, my love, until the swirling breeze

catches my breath and I breathe no more. Fly away!

On Fields of Green

July 2005

On fields of green, where I sat weeping,

I met you there, the daisies peeping...on fields of green.

Going home, you gave me hope; you gave me kisses...on

fields of green.

We shared our love, our dreams, our fears,

It was hard to hide my sombre tears...on fields of green.

I said goodbye, I set you free.

Fly away; don't think of me.

I'm confused with the love I feel for you.

Now the poppies dance where the daisies grew...on fields

of green.

If Only to Sleep

April 11, 2007

If only to sleep, if only to dream,

to escape the voices, the sounds,

the shadows moving around me.

To remember him, to hold a clear thought...

Just to open my arms and welcome him in.

Yes, my love, I know you're around me.

Was It You?

2006

Was it you who lay beside me when I felt so alone,

when I felt confused and prayed for an answer?

Was it you?

I hadn't realized when I called out your name.

I was so...blind.

Was it you?

I felt so abandoned, and there you were, right beside me.

You touched me, and your spirit touched my soul.

Those words, that feeling...

It was then that I knew: It had to be you...

Sheet of Glass

2006

The cold wind blows as I hold my old, grey, wool coat

up tight against me,
and I look, with one hand pressed against a sheet of
glass.
Though it may not be there,
I look at you.

The outline of your face: soft, worn, so...different.
I trace the details with my eyes, not realizing you have

begun to sing.

I cannot forget your lips, your smile, your kiss...
You are exactly how I should have expected you to be.

It was only your spirit I could see.

I never knew you when I thought I did—

not the man who lives so much like his father.

When did you become satisfied with that?

I wanted so much to free you from that trap.

When I gave you up, I thought I had.

I thought you were ready to fly away.

Who broke your wings, my love?

Who made you fall?

So there he sang before me, as if behind a sheet of glass.

He couldn't see me, but I saw him for the very first time:

older and wiser.

He sang and played the music he loved so much, in the

same unconscious dream he always drifted into.

Who broke your wings and made you fall?

It Makes My Heart Bleed

2006

I have so much love for you; it makes my heart bleed.

It was such a long time ago when he came,

but I cannot sleep without feeling his breath brush

against my cheek,

his body close beside me.

My heart aches; it weighs heavy when I dream of him.

Adrenalin pumps through my veins when I recall his

face...

It's just a fleeting glance, and then it's gone.

Oh, how I long for a moment—

just a moment to be near him again,

to touch, to kiss, just to know how it feels...

It makes my heart bleed.

Beyond the Door

2007

Cold, dark, black, madness...

I hope I'll never know what secret lies beyond the door,
beyond its creaking hinges.
Whoever lurks beyond that empty space, I fear.
They haunt my dreams; my sanity.
They lead me farther and farther into the unknown,
towards painted, putrid portraits, pictures dark and
ugly.

To sleep would be a luxury.
I cannot slumber, for fear of my own thoughts,
or—worse still— what secrets hide beyond the door.

I'll See You in Heaven

2006

Are you really there?

Do you lie beside me, touching me when I'm asleep?

Is it your breath I feel brushing against my cheek?

I want it to be true, but I cannot bear the consequences.

I need to know.

But surely death isn't all that's needed to make it

possible.

Doesn't God move in mysterious ways?

It cannot mean you're not alive anymore.

You were there for me when I needed you before.

Well...maybe you've found a way,

or maybe I've willed you to me somehow.

The signs you have given me have persuaded me to

believe it's you:

the door, the music, and the words you spoke;

then the noise at the window. It all fell into place.

I'm sorry I was scared,

that I had to tell you to go.

But I want you to know I'm grateful you came.

I had to send you away for the sake of my sanity,

but I love you with all my heart.

So now, my love, goodbye...

   ...and maybe I'll see you someday...in heaven.

A Love Lost in Time

February 2007

Haunting faces, fleeting glances...

I sense his death and fear the truth.

I cast a spell and will his soul to come to me.

I'm lonely and bewildered.

Please sense my presence. Please find me.

On fields of green, where I sat weeping,

I met you there, the daisies peeping.

Eight and twenty years ago it was.

I'll search for you until the swirling breeze catches my

breath, until I breathe no more.

So Brave You Are

September 2014

For such a long time, you were just a memory,

no more than a laugh, a smile.

I couldn't picture your face.

They told me you were lost, dead.

Now here you are, returned.

So brave you are.

Your clothes are smart.

Your face is solemn.

When did your smile go?

Your bed is dressed...

with flowers.

What a splendid celebration!

What a welcome home.

When they found him, his rifle lay across his body,

clutched tightly in his hands.

They could hardly prise them away.

I guess it was too much.

All that time, you lay there alone in a pool of blood.

I thought you were in Heaven.

Your eyes were closed.

I cannot forget them.

They were always so blue.

"How lucky you were," they said.

"The bullet didn't mark your face."

And now you lie in a wooden casket,

a cloth draped over the polished wood.

Upon it: a wreath of flowers, red,

like the pool of blood, they found beneath you.

I cannot look. I cannot look below...

The soil is dark and wet. Your eyes... Your eyes cannot

see.

There is no air to breathe.

You'll be cold, my love. You'll be cold tonight.

To Wake

September 2014

To wake amidst the dark of night,

to hear bombs and screams and flashes bright...
a pounding heart, a beating drum,
a cold, hot sweat, a loaded gun.

I'll never forget the way he died,
The things he said and the way he cried.
At night, I try to sleep, to dream,
but every time, I hear him scream.
"He's lost", they said, but he was dead,
in the dry, hard soil,
his earthly bed.

Those Who Are Left Behind

September 2014

Where the flowers grow, you lay your head,

beneath the soft mound of dry earth, deep,

without breath,

without air to breathe,

deserted... alone.

A boy holding out his hands:

lost, weak, shaking with fear,

unable to speak,

his lips unable to grasp the words.

Silence...

I held him in my arms.

Tears ran down my cheeks.

I turned away from the sound of the babies' cries,

but the children's begging eyes looked up at me.

Through the door I ran: free!

Hidden graves beneath my feet.

Their innocent faces haunt my dreams...

Those who are left behind.

The End

The Author

J T Bennett lives in Lincolnshire, England. *Pillars of Sand* is her first published book of poetry. She has also penned a fantasy series, Four Corners. The first instalment in that series *The Rock Star,* has been published.

Author's website; http//jtbennettauthor.wix.com/fourcorners